I0390465

BOSS GIRLS IN THE BOARDROOM

How strategy can boost your empire

Raychelle Meyers

ISBN: 1519271840
ISBN 13: 9781519271846

TABLE OF CONTENTS

ACKNOWLEDGMENTS

This book is dedicated to:

Mary Parker, Mom, you are, and always have been the boss girl in my life, since birth. Even as an adult you still boss me around- from time to time. Lol! But, I'm happy you taught me to be confident, fearless, and grateful. You don't hold back on how you feel, you're straight forward, and you take care of business. You exhibit all the characteristics of a #BossGirl. You taught me good honey, Thank you mom!

The Late Rosemary McDowell, Mother-in-Law, whom I had the privilege to call mom, may you rest in peace. For 18 years, I've admired your love for serving others. You inspired me to serve others with excellence, dignity, and respect. Your loyalty to help others transported to my spirit and motivated me step up my game. Thank you for being a woman of excellent taste and for loving, accepting, and treating me as your own daughter.

Shanna Shakir, my personal assistant, you are indeed a blessing to me and my family. Through the years, you have made it possible for me to complete important projects and take care of personal business. You rock girl and I appreciate you more than you know.

INTRODUCTION

Boss Girl! You did it! You have learned to stop settling for less and no longer give up so easily. You now stand in power among the countless women entrepreneurs who are dedicated to helping you to reach your goals and take your business to the next level. Yes, you stand wearing your bad girl boardroom suit. You enter your boardroom, where members and committee teams have you under a microscope. And mirrored in their eyes as they look into your face, you see your own reflection of excellence, confidence, professionalism, equality, and integrity. You have arrived. Okay, maybe you're still a little bit human and not a total robot…but don't tell that to your kids (who finally have a hero they can really count on)! And above all, you show appreciation and gratitude to everyone, because their unending support alongside your tenacious efforts has made you the Boss Girl that you are. You have become and are the Boss Girl you always knew you had in you.

Remember when I said, "Yes, you stand, wearing your bad girl boardroom suit?" Well, that is because this eBook will show you how to rock the strategic plan that works specifically for your business.

Making use of strategies is the #1 way female entrepreneurs achieve higher results and make their business goals a reality. This book will help you discover the power of defining the purpose of your business. It will walk you through how to design your mission statement to answer one question: *what do you accomplish for your clients?* It will give you the wisdom to predict your company's future trends and determine the direction in which it is headed. By assimilating strategic planning into your business plan, you will not only increase your profits...You will also gain more confidence and become the go-to Pro in your industry.

Boss Girl in the Boardroom is a powerful business tool written specifically to help women entrepreneurs like you obtain valuable skills in employing strategic planning. It aims to help you understand that using strategies deliver a level of success that empowers you to excel your business and increase your profits. This book was written to challenge you, shape your character, and help you gain the confidence needed to lead. It is written to help you execute your strategic plan by putting it into action.

Warning! This book is not for lazy people; you must be willing to put in time if you have a strong desire to grow your business. Strategic planning takes an ample investment of time and energy but once it is put into action, the results of your investment will pay off big time.

You know the saying...

Patience is a virtue.

Well, I can say from experience it's the truth and nothing but the truth. So, rise up girlfriend and get busy preparing for your million-dollar company!

Your results from reading this book, like those of my many clients, include many benefits.
You will gain the knowledge to establish certainty of direction: to know where your company is headed. You will be able to support your lifestyle, your family responsibilities, and your dreams by creating longevity in your business, and you will be able to contribute to society with your increased profitability. You will see massive business growth. You will be a role model to all who come after you because you will feel more confident about what you do. You will achieve success and see unparalleled results when using the strategy in this book.

But it may not always be easy.

When they first started, many of my customers faced a lot of obstacles.
They realized that they didn't think about how their competition may affect their business. They struggled because they did not get some type of funding or business loan and then found that using their own money was killing their personal account. They learned the hard lesson that the struggle was real because they felt there was nothing unique or different about their service or products. They didn't think about having a strategic plan at all, they didn't even carry out researches first so as to develop a quality financial strategic plan. They also felt like they were doing everything alone and that they had no team and no support. They were overwhelmed and felt alone.

But they didn't let their fears, worries or even their doubts or lack of knowledge stop them. They learned and implemented the skills found in this book. They learned from others in their industry and in the business industry at large. They, like you, were not willing to settle for less. They were not willing to let their struggles define and limit their capabilities.

But don't take my word for it! Yes, my clients mean the world to me and I truly appreciate every one of them. So, let them tell you their experiences with working with me to catapult their businesses in their own words:

Raychelle is just that "Ray" of sunshine that has spoken confidence, motivation, and a "Ray" of hope into the heart of everyone in her presence including me. She is and will always be my inspiration, professionally and personally. Miste M. Anders-Clemons

Many thanks for all your help and advice in helping me start my first child care business. Without your expertise, I would still be working in Corporate America. Today, I am in control of my own destiny and happy to be running my own successful business. Raychelle has been an inspiration and blessing to my business. C. Penn

I highly recommend working with Raychelle Meyers. She has trained my staff to provide the highest quality of service. She improved my company's customer service. She has given me the tools I need to take my company to the next level. Thank you Raychelle! Ashley G.

While it pleases me to provide help to such amazing Boss Girls, I sure didn't start out where I am now.

In fact, my story was not always a success and my passion and dedication to helping women entrepreneurs create millions for their businesses, comes from the heart and from that place of struggle and challenge. I struggled for **4 years** when I started my first child care business back in 1998. Struggle does not really define it. I struggled. I stumbled. I fell hard.

I did not plan well (or much at all, really) before starting the business and though I tried to make it work and was good at what I did, despite all efforts, it closed down in the 4th year. It was devastating. I watched all that hard work vanish and did not know what to do with that perceived "failure."

BUT THEN, a few years later, my mentor helped me develop a strategic plan to start another business.

It was hard to learn how to utilize the plan. I was not used to the structure and discipline. There were things I did not understand. I had to ask questions and I had to get out of my own way and commit to learning a system. So instead of wallowing in my "failure" or refusing to learn the skills it would take to start over, I put in the work.

I buckled down and created a plan that would work and it has been very successful for 9 years. I learned that this newfound success was no accident. It was not luck. And it was not even about hard work, as I had worked very hard with my first business. No, it was about that all-important **strategic plan.** I realized that I had not failed. I had simply tried to accomplish my goals without the proper tools. Now, I had found the right tools and it taught me that I can do anything, with the right strategy. This is my hope for you.

Let's bust a few MYTHS

Myth: Productivity is a goal.

> Buster- Productivity is important because it is about getting things done. However, it is the strategic planning that takes "getting things done" and turns it into getting it done *well*.

Myth: Strategic thinking is only about thinking.

> Buster- While thinking is the first step, it cannot stand on its own. Ultimately, the goal must be to put those thoughts into action. The strategic leader steps up to give the team their focus.

Myth: Execution means sticking to the plan.

Buster- A plan is not reality. It is only a concept until the strategy is put into place and the plan to be executed.

YOUR GUIDE TO STRATEGIC PLANNING

Remember that YOU we described on the first page? That **Boss Girl** who can move mountains, elicit respect upon entering the room? That woman who can proudly look in the mirror and know that she has done the very best for her family and herself? That brilliant entrepreneur who is in the process of leaving behind a great legacy that will follow her throughout the generations? Well, she read this book and she applied the following concepts without hesitation, despite any fear, and with wholeness of heart. *Boss Girl in the Boardroom* consists of the following topics. May you enjoy these short chapters and may they serve you on your Boss Journey!

It is critical to your success and the success of your business to learn and implement strategic planning. You must determine your goals for the business. Use a method when making this determination – the SMART goal method: your goals should be **S**pecific, **M**easurable, **A**ttainable, **R**ealistic, and have a **T**ime period attached to them. Write down your goals so that you can review and revise them as needed while you are evaluating your business' strategic process. In the next few sections, you will be given specific ideas on how to use this strategy to grow your business. To have a well-developed and executed strategic plan means that you will, in turn, develop a competitive advantage.

As you go through the principles in this book, you may find it helpful to keep a special notebook just for all the ideas and strategies that you will discover. This is your guide to producing the most affective vehicle to freedom you may ever create: a business that is insanely profitable, a community that depends on you and on whom you depend, and freedom to pursue a lifestyle that fills you, your family, and loved ones with joy. Please set aside all distractions as you peruse this book for the first time and give it your whole attention.

BOSS GIRLS: BE UNIQUE

Understanding the competition is crucial. It is this understanding that will give you the inspiration to purposely create something unique about your company that makes you stand out from your competitors. This is your chance to be different with regards to your branding, services, products, and even your marketing style. Find the qualities that excel and focus all your energy in those areas. Fill in the gap. By studying your competitors, you will discover what they are not offering or doing and this will give you ideas of where you can provide a much better service for your clients. It never hurts to do a little research. Knowledge is power my friends.

When studying your competitors, look at their branding. What does it say about them? What are their beliefs and what drives them? How does it differ from your branding? What makes your branding, your mission, more memorable? What do you stand for that they do not? What separates you from the pack? Branding is the greatest way to put a stamp on all your unique qualities so be sure not to overlook this vital tool.

As for their services, how does yours differ? What do you offer that they do not? What ways of showing appreciation and handling customer care do you provide that goes above and beyond what your industry expects? If your competitors have a similar product, what makes yours better or more valuable? What can you offer with each product to enhance its perceived value in the marketplace? What guarantees do you give?

Lastly, what is your competitors' marketing style? What type of clients does it draw? How can you tweak your marketing to attract ONLY those clients who are your ideal clients? Think about your messaging, word usage, even the colors on your website and marketing materials. How do these elements resonate with your ideal clients?

As you begin your discovery session, take special note of the qualities in which you excel and focus all your energy in these areas. Remember the 80/20 rule? It's the one that states that 20% of your efforts will result in 80% of your results. So, look deeply into those areas of excellence. You will undoubtedly find that sharp, razor focus on those areas lead to greater results with higher accuracy. When something works, repeat it! Find *what* made it work and focus on that one point. This practice will go a long way towards helping you to achieve your goals quickly and with seeming effortlessness.

Filling in the gap does not mean you sell out and just do the things that no one wants to do. It means that you see the areas that are not being addressed and exploring the possibilities. For example, maybe your competitor provides a great service but they don't always follow up with answers in their FB chat. That is your cue to make sure that you do follow up with your clients. Sometimes, there is a gap because there is no market for the intended service or product. In this case, it's okay to leave that gap and concentrate on others. If you have the time and funding, it is, however, a good idea to test that theory first. It may be that competitors just haven't found the right marketing tool. And you may be the first to penetrate that space.

Above all, remember to be unique. There is only ever going to be one you. Even if your service or product seems like a dime a dozen or you think that your market is saturated, remember what Jeff Walker says about people coming to you for your "content" but staying for the connection. In this case, your services or products may be what they are coming for but either way, they will stay because of the unique way you present them. They will stay because they like you and all your unique qualities. So, own them, Boss Girl!

BOSS GIRLS: KNOW YOUR PURPOSE

To know the purpose of your business is to implement a detailed plan on how you will solve a problem for your customers. It begins with a simple, yet powerful mission statement. Your mission statement is designed to answer the question, "what you are trying to accomplish for your customers?" This is the most important question you will ever ask and it is very important to shine the spotlight on the needs your company serves.

To really answer this question thoroughly, there are several trending exercises you can do. You can create your avatar. Avatars are your absolute ideal clients. You will describe them as people that you know. Another exercise can be to simply list what challenges your clients face. What keeps them up at night with worry that your product or service can help them with? What are their dreams, aspirations? Why do they struggle with their problems? What sort of solutions, besides yours, have they tried to implement and how did it work for them? What makes your solution worth the try? Whether you use an Avatar or just write the list, this work is CRITICAL for the success of your business.

Then write out their beliefs. What do they believe in? What do they care most about? What values do they care deeply about? What causes do they support and where do they invest their time? How do their beliefs align with yours? What are their habits? What is their lifestyle? All these bits of information give you great insight into the hearts of your clients.

How do you find this information? Well, you can do it the old-fashioned way and pick up the phone and call them. Ask them if they would do you a favor and spare just 5 or 10 minutes of their time and ask if "now" is a good time. If so, continue and if not, ask them if you could call them back at another date. Let them know that you are working on an upcoming project and that their input would mean the world to you. Then simply ask them questions by framing each one within the parameters of your expertise. Be sure to write down their exact words.

For example, if you sell coffee mugs, ask them what struggles they may have concerning how to keep from dropping and shattering their pretty World Market mug...3 times! *Yes, that would be me...* Ask them why they want reusable mugs (of course, they may say something along the lines of saving the planet, but you really can push for greater details). The idea is to find out their struggles and problems *in their language* so that you can speak to them *in their language* when you market or post on social media.

Armed with this information, write out your mission statement in the standard, "I help x do y so that they can z." This will be the foundation of your mission statement. You can definitely expand on this or you can keep it super simple. Then, be sure to include what you believe in and copy the Apple Example: Lots of what you believe in and end with something along the lines of, "and by the way, I also happen to sell unbreakable, sustainable coffee mugs – that are super pretty."

BOSS GIRLS: VISUALIZE THE FUTURE

A strategic vision is the image of a company's future and the direction it is headed. Think big! What will your business look like in 5 to 10 years from now? For women entrepreneurs to stay competitive, we must be more strategic and more effective in anticipating important market changes. We must think in multiples such as producing an action plan for the possible future that leads to providing multiple services. It's important to remember that you just can't talk about it – you must talk about it and *be* about it. The more you speak into the future of your business, the more creative you can be about planning and budgeting for the possibilities of growth a few years from now.

Your business in 5 years. 10 years. What does it look like? Where is, it headed? Think about why you started this business in the first place. What were your dreams? What was your purpose? In five or ten years, will you have completed the level of accomplishment you thought you would? How does your company serve the community?

How does it serve your family's financial and philanthropic needs? How does it help you on your mission to becoming a better person? It is important to remember that no one starts a business with the hopes that it will fail. By not visualizing your company five and ten, even twenty or thirty years in the future, haven't you already doomed it to failure?

Now think of Apple again. "1000 songs in your pocket" has turned into practically a small entertainment center in your pocket, along with several different kinds of desktops and laptops, iPhones and iWatches, and a plethora of other devices and accessories. Without your vision of a "suite" of products and/or services, your business may become stagnant and fall behind the curve, especially in today's market. Your clients want fresh, new, and even repurposed and reinvented products and/or services from you. By continuing to create for them, you show them your dedication to their needs and create mad, raving fans. Plus, you will make a little money, and that never hurts.

Plan that future. Talk about it and *be* about it. Always look for ways to expand and grow. Budget accordingly and yes, have a business savings account along with a projected budget for reinvesting into your company with education and innovation. Keep active plans and act on those plans regularly, that way they do not become pipe dreams or fantasies. Turn your deepest desires into reality. Remember, a plan not acted on is like planting a seed and not watering it. It is only *action* that can bring life and hope to any plan and no matter how far off the goal is, daily or weekly action is the only way to keep it alive, even if it is just very small, easy tasks.

An example of this is, say that your coffee mug business is doing well and you have decided to start a small kiosk at the mall during the holidays. In this kiosk, you will not only sell your pretty, world famous mugs, you will also sell coffee. But you've no idea how to be a barista. You can begin studying now; maybe even get a job in a coffee shop (not for money, but for the experience). You could travel to different places that produce the coffee bean, get to know suppliers, etc. You could even write a short tutorial on brewing that perfect cup of coffee at home (as if, am I, right? But it would make a perfect opting offer!). So, the first week might be a task as simple as Googling different types of coffee beans. Then you might start going to coffee shops. Of course, you probably already frequent them regularly. In that case, start making friends with the owner and baristas. Make sure you are know when they are hiring.

As you can see, planning is the birth of the baby or the planting of the seed and it is far easier to keep it alive with small, consistent actions. So, get planning that future and then get acting on that plan.

BOSS GIRLS: EVALUATE YOUR COMPANY

Use a SWOT analysis to discover your company's **S**trengths, **W**eaknesses, **O**pportunities, and **T**hreats. This analysis will help you to look more closely at your business and provide guidance to help produce a good fit between your company's strengths and its opportunities. Evaluate the success of your business strategic plan by surveying your employees, customers, and business associates. You can ask questions of specific people and create an online survey to get anonymous responses from these important parties to your business. Review your financial component, risk assessment, personnel and marketing skills, and support, as well to ensure you have the necessary background to make a success of your new venture.

The SWOT analysis is a highly-used tool to really get into the core of your organization. All sorts of companies, organizations, municipalities, and institutions have used it. While for years, most people believed that it was created by American business consultant, Albert S. Humphrey, he emphatically claimed in his published paper before his death in 2005, that he was not the creator. Now other claims are cropping up, but whoever the creator is, the work remains the same.

It delves into these four major aspects of your company and for the sake of trying to give you more with less, I have included lesser known ideas rather than the many obvious points floating around on the Ethernets:

- Strengths. Your #1 strength is your employees (unless they suck, in which case that would be your #1 weakness). What is your level of commitment to them? Do you pay them enough that they can relax on their day off? Do you listen to their concerns and train them with patience as needed? Now consider customer relations. Are you giving your customers an "experience" every single time they come into your shop or visit your website or FB page? Count your connections. How many of them would really have your back in time of need and vice-versa?
- Weaknesses. While many hate this category, it really is a great one because it supplies fuel to spark your strategic goals. Improvement is always a good thing and the only mistake people make here, is not admitting their true weaknesses for fear of discovery. Write a comprehensive list and know that you can use this list as a guide for furthering your education.
- Opportunities. Always look for "opportunities" to serve others first. We can head back to our list of connections and find ways to serve them. Once you have exhausted all the opportunities to serve, then you can go into the more traditional view of counting what opportunities you can

capitalize on. You will find that this small mind shift will open doors to even greater opportunities.

- Threats. Are your offers in line with what people want? If not, they are your company's most powerful threat because without them, your business cannot make money. Who are your enemies? Don't say anyone. *Someone* does not like you. And that's okay. List them here. Some of your "weaknesses" may pose a threat to the organization. List them here as well.

The conclusion is to then compile all the information and create your list of obtainable strategic goals. Include a timeline for completion along with definitive and measurable actions that will serve as milestones to the realization of that goal. You can also use the information you received from the aforementioned surveys and interviews to mold and tweak your goals or strategic plan.

And of course, always be on guard with your financials, marketing, and education. Know what money there is and where it's coming from even if it is not your strong point. Take a business accounting class to familiarize yourself with your books. You can always hire someone to keep track of financials and even provide advice. But best to do so only AFTER you know your way around a calculator. Fine tune your offers and always be learning.

BOSS GIRLS: STUDY YOUR CUSTOMERS

S trategic planning can also help you study your customers. After all, your customers are the lifelines of your business, or you wouldn't have one. If you want to upgrade your company from being successful to being ridiculously profitable, then you need to meet your customers' needs better than your competitors do. You also need to create lasting memories and experiences for and with them. This is where your earlier work in creating your Avatar comes in handy! Now that you know what drives him or her, you can fine-tune your strategy to serve even better.

Here are 9 of the highest recommended tips to get you started:

1. You must act upon maintaining the customer's lifestyle. How does your product or service best give consistent and reliable service that supports your customer's quality of life (and, more specifically, their *way of life*)? Make sure your company is a perfect complement to their standards.

2. Look past the purchase. The purchase is the first real step with regards to your customer joining your company's family. Treat them like royalty! Find ways to say thank you. Carrie Glenn, founder of Etiquette at Hand, teaches her clients that there are "never too many ways to say thank you and nary an inappropriate time to show appreciation."
3. See the person and not their money. This is big. Imagine going to a car lot and feeling the urge to hide from the salesman. This is not the feeling you want to inadvertently create in your customers. By seeing *them* and not their pocket book, you create a relationship based on trust. Keep in mind that old saying: people buy from those they know, like and trust.
4. Use all available data and think like a big company. For a lot of new business owners, this can be a tough one. Here's the thing. If you don't have the skills, hire it done. Get someone on your team trained. This is vital to the ongoing success in today's industry.
5. Gain access to crafting customer communication and online web data to learn their style, taste, or brand. Again, use a professional if you don't know how to do this.
6. Keep track and learn past purchase behavior and spending habits of each customer. There are many ways to do this and if you don't know how, at the risk of repeating myself, hire an expert to help you.
7. It's always a good idea to contact the customer before they contact you. Check in from time to time. Let them know you are working on your project or that a new item has come in or give them first dibs on an upcoming sale. Let them know that you are thinking of them and their needs.
8. Identify customer triggers and the time of the year they are likely to spend more. This goes a long way towards serving your client best. Don't just assume that Christmas or

Valentine's Day will be the hopping times of year. Your ideal customer may shop for Christmas in September. She or he may have children who are students, which could mean they spend more as a family during the summer months. This valuable information will serve not only your customer, but you!

9. Social media, loyalty cards, customer appreciation month, are all great ways to keep your customers returning. Again, back to the "thank you." Did you know that the greatest way to say, "Thank you," to someone who has any social media presence is to like, comment on, and share their posts? This is especially true if they have a FB page or a business Twitter account. So, get sharing, reposting, commenting, retweeting, double tapping...all in the name of good business! And of course, remember to appreciate them with gifts and recognition.

BOSS GIRLS: CREATE GOALS & OBJECTIVES

Goals and objectives are fast tracks to your mission and vision. While some goals may (and sometimes should be) broad and global in nature, your immediate goals should be measurable, quantifiable, and supported by your objectives. Objectives set the agenda and are the specific steps you will use to accomplish your goals. Make sure both goals and objectives build on your company's strengths and opportunities. This approach can also keep your employees focused and on track, which can give you the added advantage of increased productivity. Focus on planning, management, staffing, measurement, and adjustment.

Goals that are measurable, quantifiable, and supported by objectives are SMART goals. Remember the characteristics of SMART goals include:

- Specific
- Measurable
- Attainable (this one seems to have been changed by others based on personal preferences to "agreed upon" or "actionable" but the original is attainable or achievable)
- Realistic
- Time Sensitive

Objectives set the agenda and are the specific steps you will use to accomplish your goals. For example, in our coffee mug illustration, remember we had an earlier goal to open a kiosk at the mall? Then we would set up our objectives to break down and put that goal into action. The objectives could include:

- Asses your market (you can even break this down further)
- Learn how to make and serve coffee
- Research kiosk size and price
- Research and buy any insurance that may be needed
- Gain support from those who can come, those who will post about it, and those who will refer others to the kiosk

Make sure both goals and objectives build on your strengths and opportunities. If you really, *really,* are terrible at customer service in a service-based situation, you might consider hiring a barista. If you don't know anything about insurance, ask your agent (or other trusted person) for advice. Focus on those objectives in which you excel and delegate all the others.

Also, make sure that you fully utilize the opportunities that are available to you as you move through the objectives. Obviously, your happy customers, friends in the community, and each new customer that approaches your kiosk all bring opportunity for your success. Opportunities will arise as you work through your objectives so keep your eyes open to them.

Share this approach, this plan, with your employees. It will help to keep them focused and on track, thus increasing productivity. Have you ever gone to an event (or even party) where you jumped in and helped and the host just didn't know up from down or what to do next? It's extremely frustrating and feels like a waste of time or at the very least, you just feel like you are in the way. Even though you may point out that your employees are being paid, the fact is, not having clear goals and objectives from which employees can execute, unfortunately, this ties their hands and prevents them from giving you their very best. So, get those goals and objectives to them and even consider allowing them to participate in creating some or all the plan if appropriate. Then sit back and watch them help you build your profits!

Develop this type of strategic plan to also help you assess your market, plan your course of action, and devise specific strategies for achieving your desired outcomes. It will also give your business an incredible advantage over competitors, especially if you are in a market that is predominately unaware of or apathetic to this approach. Many small and home businesses do not really follow this approach. This gives you the authority to brand yourself as an expert in your industry. It also gives you an "opportunity" to perhaps create a training course for your competitors. This creates an immediate atmosphere of camaraderie and promotes reciprocity and can even be a stepping stool for unifying your competitors and ultimately boosting profits.

BOSS GIRLS: TAKE ACTION

Take action. This means having a dedicated team who shares your same passion about the business. Magic happens when a team of people come together for a great cause to achieve a certain goal or task. This happens with great force and accomplishment; thus, the team is not divided; they are dedicated to the mission and will not stop until the mission is complete. This is the type of team every entrepreneur dreams of. With strategic planning, it's important to act and run with it. Everybody should be focused on one word, **ACTIVATE**. Assign responsibilities and deadlines to ensure implementation. A great method is to assign each staff with a specific goal. Have them write their individual plan and be responsible for making sure each task is accomplished.

Taking action means being brave. It does NOT mean "not being afraid." The difference is that bravery is not the absence of fear. Bravery is facing the fear and acting anyway. For those of you who find it difficult to take action, one recommendation is to keep a list of what you did, thought, or studied in those times when you procrastinated taking action. These insights could give you a glimpse into what your motivating factor is. For example, if you were going to pick up the phone and make calls and instead, you watched the latest sales training webinar, that is a clear indicator that you are TERRIFIED to make calls. And one quick side note on this:

EVERYONE IS TERRIFIED TO MAKE CALLS

I'm sorry but it's true. At least 99.99999999999999999999999 9999% of the time. And here's the kicker. While many MLM professionals earn an average of about $60,000 per year, studies show that when an MLM marketer chooses to

LOVE
making calls

and *forces* him or herself to enjoy the process, his or her annual income will jump to a starting point of around $240,000 per year. That is a 400% raise for just making yourself love making sales calls.

So how do you force yourself to love making sales calls? Well, remember my good friend and fellow Etiquette Expert, Carrie Glenn? She also studies ballet. Here's the thing, though. She came to it late – in her late 30s, overweight, out of shape, and not nearly as flexible as anyone else. (Don't worry! She gave me permission to tell her story!)

Well, for those of you who may not know, one section of barre work is called "Adagio." It consists of long, agonizingly slow, and painful lifts of each leg in every possible direction and held up in the air in impossible positions for what Carrie would describe as, "an eternity." She hated them. They made her feel fat, ugly and incompetent. They hurt and never, *ever* seemed to improve.

Then one day, one of her teachers joked about how little kids always have to go to the bathroom during Adagios. Carrie asked why and was told that it was because they hated them and wanted to get out of doing them. It was in this moment, that Carrie realized that, while quite normal and socially accepted, her feelings of hate towards this barre exercise would have to mature and even dissipate. She decided to try an experiment.

At every class from that moment forward, when it was time for Adagios, Carrie would announce to anyone who would listen that she *loved* Adagios and that this was her favorite part of barre. She told herself that very same lie. She pictured herself onstage, dancing in full costume and lights and with a handsome prince behind her (of course...). She embraced the exercise and made it fun and one day stopped caring whether or not her leg would ever go as high as her amazing teacher. It would go a tiny bit higher than the year before and the year before that and that was the point. As long as she worked on it, she got better.

Carrie cannot tell when the change happened. But to this day, Adagios are her favorite part of barre. The kicker (if you will pardon the pun) is that she never really improved all that much in this area of her dance studies and is at a similar level as when she first started. Maybe a little better. While this practice did not improve her capabilities – only hard work in the studio will do that – it did change the way she feels about Adagios.

You can apply this same technique to make yourself love making phone calls (or going to networking events or whatever is in business that scares you). Tell yourself how excited you are as you prepare. Make up stories and scenarios if you must. Do what it takes to force yourself into taking action. Action really is where your business begins and ends. Be sure that you do not short-change yourself in this area.

TIPS FOR SUCCESS!!Before you stop reading this book and start taking action on the pearls of wisdom found herein, be sure to follow these tips for success:

a. Be willing to try something different and unique that may allow your business to skyrocket. Not every great idea comes in a neat little package. Keep your eyes and yourself open to suggestions, particularly if they make you uncomfortable.

b. Always follow through and execute your strategic plan even if you think it will not work. Do it! The only way that you will know if your plan works is to put it into action and the only way you will know what needs to be improved is by measuring data during the process of putting it into action. Listen, sometimes the scariest part of business is making the decision to pull the trigger on a particular purchase or action. We all face this fear and, Boss Girl, you are worth the effort! Your business is worth taking chances. If the worse that can happen is that it doesn't work, then you can always try something else. This is your time, so go grab that big brass ring.

c. Trust your instincts. If you learn nothing else from this book, always trust your instincts. They will always guide you in the right direction. Even when things don't work, all the actions you take will positively impact all future strategies.

d. Do not be afraid to ask for help if you're uncertain about something. Ask your successful business mentors, your friends (who know what they are talking about), even me! Remember, you can always shoot me a message on my FB page:

https://www.facebook.com/raychellemeyers/?ref=bookmarks

I do my best to answer all messages. You can also find amazing tips and tricks there, so pop on over any time and join the conversation! Also, you can reach out to your local Chamber of Commerce, Rotary Club...the options for support are endless so please reach out. Remember, we all started out NEW. We all had to ask what seems to us to be millions of questions. Remember that your question could actually help someone else too.

e. Develop a team who share your passion... it's okay to express it's not about you, but the company mission. They need to see your genuine side.

What if...

You followed every bit of advice in this book? What if you took your business, regardless of the fact that it's a new or old, profitable or floundering, and applied these principles to your infrastructure? Chances are, you would find marked improvement and profits because you would gain more thrilled and loyal customers. You would make more money. You would increase your confidence and your competence. You would gain more respect from others and have a deeper respect for yourself. What about your family?

How would their lives be impacted by your business expertise? Would they come to you for advice and maybe actually follow it (to some degree anyway, lol)? Would they grow closer to you because success will eventually give you more free time to spend with them? Will you actually be able to give them the skills they will need later in life when it's time for them to leave the nest and find their own way? What better gift to give your children?

What if your journey leads you to being more professional and to always show common courtesy to all customers...and employees, colleagues, and even your family? Can you even imagine the ease of getting through major conflicts when you address and respond to everyone with civility and respect? It's easy to have respect and another thing entirely to commit to always "showing" respect. As your confidence levels grow, it is easier to "BE" in your own skin and that makes every conflict just a little bit easier to handle.

And what if you always knew every aspect of your business? What if you could see the upcoming trends and therefore be able to strategize for success around those trends? What if you began attending business classes or workshops? What if you revamped your branding? What if you *nailed* those online ads on social media and those sequenced launches? How would that affect your business? How excited would you be to jump out of bed and get to work each day? How hard would it be to tear yourself away, but then the moment you do and you find yourself actually relaxing or hanging with friends and loved ones, you don't have to worry because you know that your business is doing great. You are walking in your purpose, supported by an ACTIONABLE AND STRATEGIC PLAN like none other!

And what would happen if you started sharing your expertise? What if you began training each of your clients on how to increase their business profits? Our economy is moving through an exciting change and strategic planning really can be a super fun activity! When you succeed, and then help others succeed, what kind of legacy are you really leaving behind?

As we near the end of our time together, take a moment to pause and reflect on these questions and any subsequent questions that arise. Jot down your thoughts and turn them into goals, throw in a few objectives, and get rolling!

Know that you are not alone. You are in the company of the most amazing BOSS GIRLS in any boardroom ever and it has been my privilege to share this bit of time together. Remember to use this book often! Pull it out when you have a question, mark it up, draw in the margins. Make this your go-to for any boardroom event.

Most importantly, when you set this book down, head on over to

http://www.raychellemeyers.com

and join a community of the most incredible Boss Girls ever by subscribing to my high content, effective, and action-packed business newsletters in which you will get the latest tips on growing your business. Take ACTION today to set your business and yourself apart.

ABOUT THE AUTHOR

 Against all odds, Raychelle Meyers accomplished a milestone of accomplishments by living her dreams despite being raised in a poverty-stricken home. She was determined to start a new trend of possibilities by taking on the challenge of breaking the curse of poverty in her family. By the age of 23, the challenge was activated when she decided to start a private child care business for busy corporate moms. Today, she comes with 25 years' experience in early childhood development.

Raychelle Meyers is the President & CEO of Apples & Oranges Corp, a youth non-profit organization that provides enrichment programs, free after-school child care, and healthy foods to at-risk and homeless youth. She oversees an operating budget of $1.1 million and manages over 50 poverty-fighting programs in Texas. The organization also empower teens to start their own businesses in their communities.

Raychelle is a transformational speaker, author, producer, and youth mentor. She's been featured in various magazines like USA Today Magazine, HD Encore Magazine, Focus on Women Magazine, just to name a few. She's been heard on a variety of radio shows across the nation and internationally. She's been a featured speaker at the University of Arlington Texas, where she shared her expertise on local child hunger and how her organization help fight hunger in communities across Texas. She was later featured in the UTA Shorthorn Newspaper. She's the author of the best-selling book, Confined Minds: Break-Free from Imprisoned Thoughts.

Raychelle's a Film Producer with Maximum Achievement DNA Films, a 4-time Emmy Award Winning Film company featuring, The Soul of Success: The Jack Canfield Story. This is her first film as a Producer.

She currently lives in the DFW area in Texas with her husband Ulysses Meyers. The couple share two adult children and two grandchildren. On her down time, she loves spending time with family, traveling, reading, writing, photography, camping, and boating.

To Hire Me Contact:
(817) 713-5202
raychellemeyers.pa@gmail.com